Score

AF905225

Suite Detroit: Sounds of an American City

For Flute, Alto Saxophone, and Piano

CATHERINE ROLLIN

Commissioned by Music Teachers National Association
for the 2018 National Conference in Orlando, Florida

When given the instrumentation for this trio, I immediately thought of my musical roots from my hometown of Detroit, Michigan. Detroit is a city that exemplifies the American spirit of innovation and invention. In the 20th century, wealth was generated in the city, primarily through the auto industry. These newly found resources led to major investments in the arts, including the Detroit Institute of Arts and the Detroit Symphony Orchestra.

I was fortunate to study with concert pianist Mischa Kottler, who came to Detroit in the 1930s and later became the principal pianist with the Detroit Symphony Orchestra. In addition to the classical piano background from lessons with Mr. Kottler, I was also influenced by other musical styles that surrounded me in the city. I heard Motown songs on the radio before they became national hits. Since Detroit was a mecca for jazz, I heard great jazz pianists such as Chick Corea, McCoy Tyner, and Oscar Peterson. While still in high school, I had the unforgettable experience of hearing Bill Evans perform his musical magic at the famous Baker's Keyboard Lounge.

In the first and third movements of this trio, I incorporated jazz influences such as syncopation and swung eighth notes. The three movements are related by key. In the jazz spirit, the flute and alto saxophone players are encouraged to explore alternate articulations in the third movement if desired. The outer movements are in D minor, and the middle movement is in F major, the relative major. All three movements briefly move into the key of D major, which functions as a ray of musical sunshine. This D major musical color reflects my hope for the continuing resurgence of Detroit and other large inner cities across America.

I am grateful to the Music Teachers National Association (MTNA) for providing me with the opportunity to write and present this trio. I am especially honored since MTNA has been a vital part of my work as a teacher, composer, and pianist for my entire professional life. I also want to thank Dr. Ann Rivers Witherspoon, National Chair for the MTNA Composer Commissioning Program, for her dedication to bringing new accessible chamber music to developing musicians. I hope this trio will provide a rewarding musical experience.

Alfred Music
P.O. Box 10003
Van Nuys, CA 91410-0003
alfred.com

ISBN-10: 1-4706-3948-3
ISBN-13: 978-1-4706-3948-8

Cover Photo:
The Renaissance Center (Detroit, MI) © Getty Images / franckreporter

Suite Detroit: Sounds of an American City

I. The City: Overture and Improvisation

Catherine Rollin

9
mp
poco cresc.
mf
mp
9
p
poco cresc.
13
mf
poco cresc.
poco rit. e dim.
mp
poco cresc.
poco rit. e dim.
13
mp
poco cresc.
poco rit. e dim.
17
a tempo
mp
poco cresc.
poco rit.
a tempo
poco rit.
17
a tempo
p
poco cresc.
poco rit.

21
Slightly faster with a lively swing feel
mp
poco cresc.
mf
p
poco cresc.
mp
25
mp
poco cresc.
mf
p
poco cresc.
mp
29
mf
poco cresc.
mp
poco cresc.
mf

33
mf
poco cresc.
f
mp
mp
poco cresc.
mf
37
f
poco cresc.
mf
poco cresc.
mp
poco cresc.
mf
41
mf
legato
mp
mp

45
f
mf
45
mf
49
mf
poco cresc.
49
mp
poco cresc.
mf
53
mp
mf
poco cresc.
f
53
mp
poco cresc.
mf

* Begin the trill on F-sharp and end it on beat 1 of measure 68.

II. Belle Isle: An Interlude

5
a tempo
mp
molto cantabile
mf
mp
3
a tempo
5
a tempo
pp
p
7
mf
poco rit.
poco rit.
7
mp
mp
poco rit.
9
a tempo
mp
mf
mp
3
a tempo
9
a tempo
pp
p

11
più appassionato
mf
f
più appassionato
mf
11
mp
mf
simile
13
mf
mp
13
mf
mp
15
f
poco rit.
mf
mp poco rit.
15
mf
mp
poco rit.

Flute

Commissioned by Music Teachers National Association
for the 2018 National Conference in Orlando, Florida

Suite Detroit: Sounds of an American City

I. The City: Overture and Improvisation

Catherine Rollin

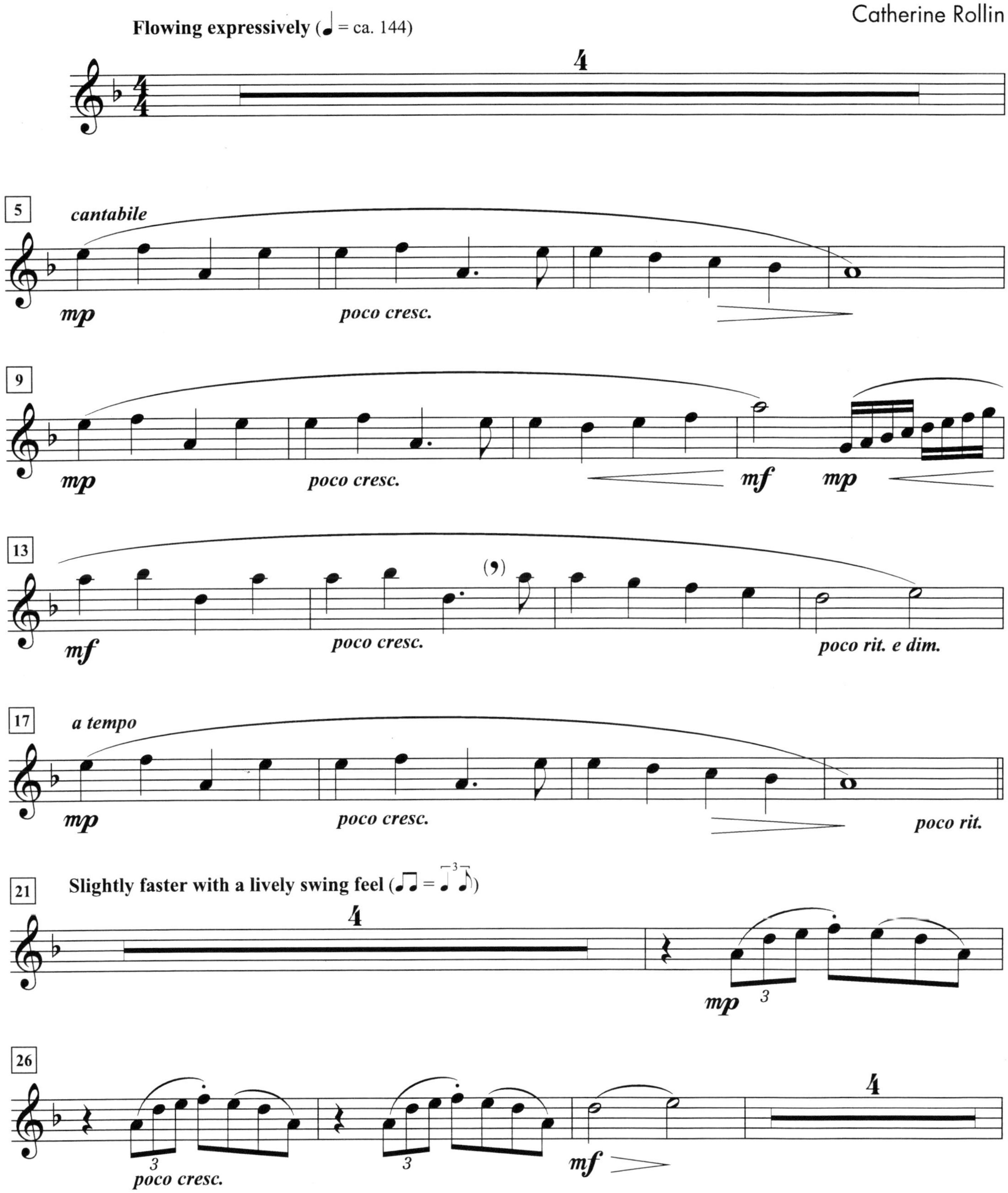

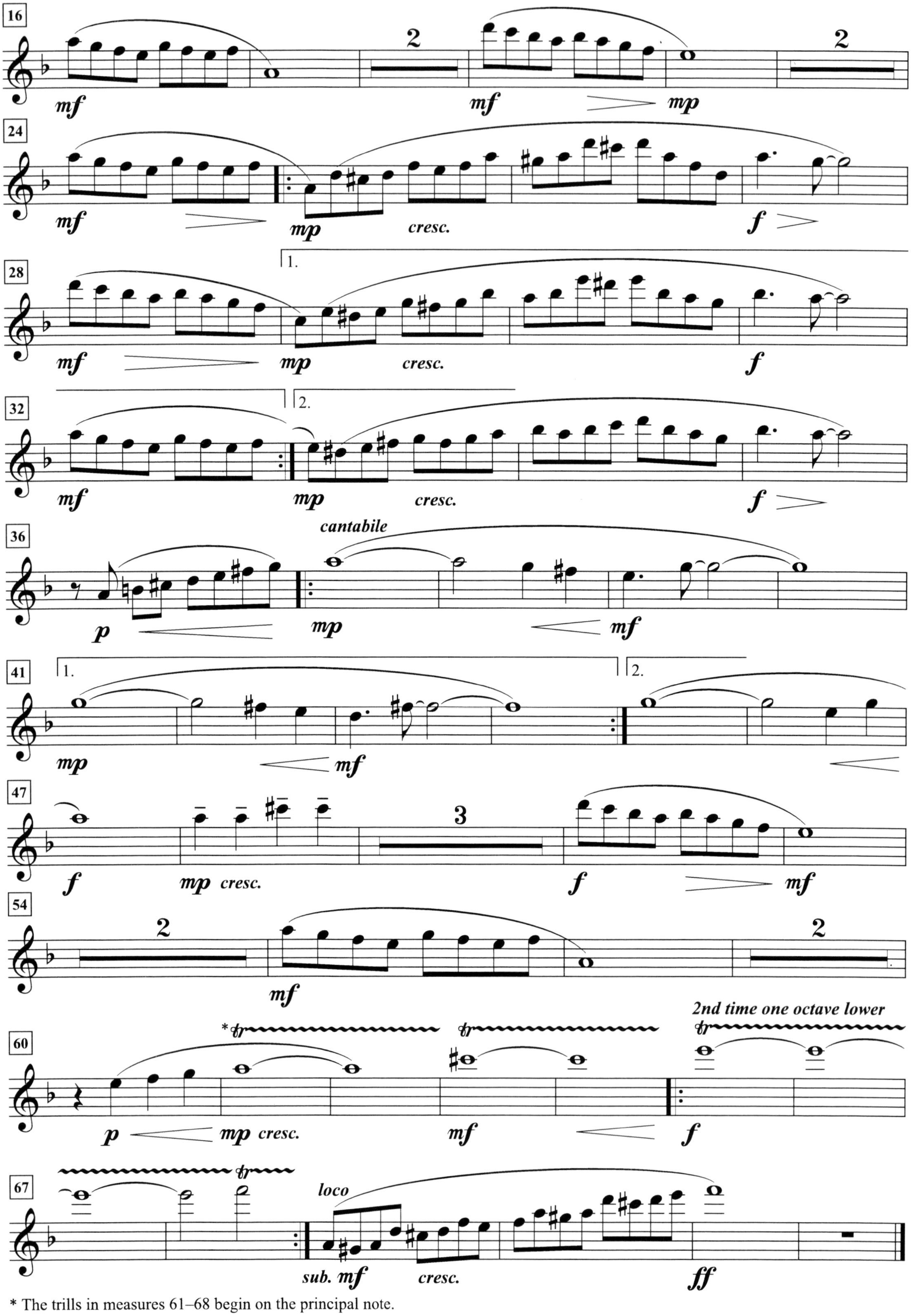

* The trills in measures 61–68 begin on the principal note.

II. Belle Isle: An Interlude

III. Good Vibes: Finale

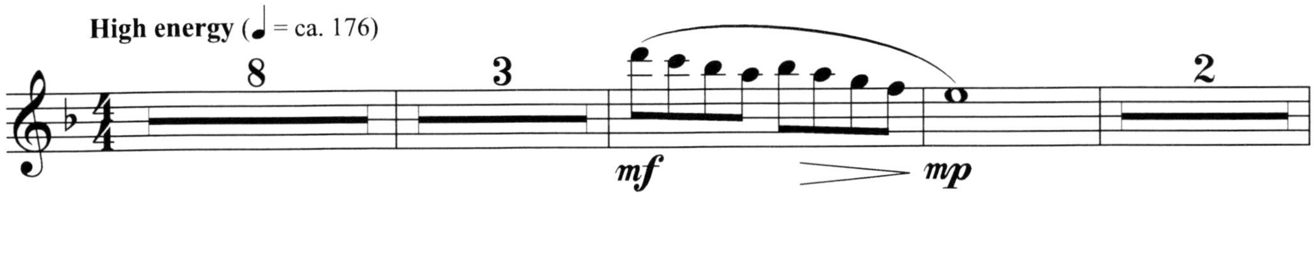

* Begin the trill on F-sharp, and end it on beat 1 of measure 68.

E♭ Alto Saxophone

Commissioned by Music Teachers National Association
for the 2018 National Conference in Orlando, Florida

Suite Detroit: Sounds of an American City

I. The City: Overture and Improvisation

Catherine Rollin

37
p
mp
41
1.
p
mp
45
2.
mf
cresc.
49
mf
cresc.
f
mf
53
mp
cresc.
f
57
mf
cresc.
f
p
61
mp
cresc.
mf
65
f
69
sub. mp
cresc.
f

III. Good Vibes: Finale

II. Belle Isle: An Interlude

17
a tempo
a tempo
singing tenderly
cresc.
mf
mp
17
a tempo
pp
p
19
a tempo
poco rit.
a tempo
mf
poco rit.
mp
cresc.
19
a tempo
mp
mp
poco rit.
pp
22
più appassionato
f
più appassionato
mf
f
mf
22
p
mp
mf
simile

25
mf
mp
25
mf
mp
27
f
mp poco rit.
mf
poco rit.
27
mp
mp
poco rit.
29
a tempo
singing tenderly
cresc.
mf
mp
a tempo
p singing tenderly
cresc.
mp
p
29
a tempo
pp
p

31
mf
rit.
a tempo
mp
mp
rit.
a tempo
p
31
p
mp
rit.
a tempo
p
34
mp
mp
rit.
p
p
rit.
34
pp
p
pp
rit.
37
meno mosso
rit.
p
meno mosso
rit.
pp
37
meno mosso
p
mp
rit.
pp

III. Good Vibes: Finale

13
mp
mp
cresc.
f
mf
13
p
cresc.
mf
mp
17
mp
cresc.
f
mf
17
p
cresc.
mf
21
mp
mp
cresc.
f
mf
21
p
cresc.
mf
mp

25
mp
cresc.
f
mf
p
mf
mp
25
p
cresc.
mf
mp
29
1.
mp
cresc.
f
mf
p
mf
mp
29
p
cresc.
mf
mp
33
2.
mp
cresc.
f
p
p
mf
33
p
cresc.
mf
mp

37
cantabile
mp
mf
p
mp
37
legato
p
mp
41
1.
mp
mf
p
mp
41
p
mp
45
2.
f
mp cresc.
mf
cresc.
45
mf

49
mf
cresc.
f
f
mf
49
mp
cresc.
mf
53
mf
mp
cresc.
f
mf
53
mp
cresc.
mf
mp
57
p
mf
cresc.
f
p
57
cresc.
mf
f

* The trills in measures 61–68 begin on the principal note.

Alfred